IF FO

MW01240507

GREATER THAN A TOURIST BOOK
SERIES
REVIEWS FROM READERS

I think the series is wonderful and beneficial for tourists to get information before visiting the city.

-Seckin Zumbul, Izmir Turkey

I am a world traveler who has read many trip guides but this one really made a difference for me. I would call it a heartfelt creation of a local guide expert instead of just a guide.

-Susy, Isla Holbox, Mexico

New to the area like me, this is a must have!

-Joe, Bloomington, USA

This is a good series that gets down to it when looking for things to do at your destination without having to read a novel for just a few ideas.

-Rachel, Monterey, USA

Good information to have to plan my trip to this destination.

-Pennie Farrell, Mexico

Great ideas for a port day.

-Mary Martin USA

Aptly titled, you won't just be a tourist after reading this book. You'll be greater than a tourist!

-Alan Warner, Grand Rapids, USA

Even though I only have three days to spend in San Miguel in an upcoming visit, I will use the author's suggestions to guide some of my time there. An easy read - with chapters named to guide me in directions I want to go.

-Robert Catapano, USA

Great insights from a local perspective! Useful information and a very good value!

-Sarah, USA

This series provides an in-depth experience through the eyes of a local. Reading these series will help you to travel the city in with confidence and it'll make your journey a unique one.

-Andrew Teoh, Ipoh, Malaysia

GREATER THAN A TOURIST – MEMPHIS TENNESSEE USA

50 Travel Tips from a Local

Claude L Chafin

Cover designed by: Ivana Stamenkovic
Cover Image: https://pixabay.com/en/memphis-tennessee-scenery-678028/

Greater Than a Tourist
Visit our website at www.GreaterThanaTourist.com

Lock Haven, PA
ISBN: 9781983270932

>TOURIST

50 TRAVEL TIPS FROM A LOCAL

BOOK DESCRIPTION

Are you excited about planning your next trip?

Do you want to try something new?

Would you like some guidance from a local?

If you answered yes to any of these questions, then this Greater Than a Tourist book is for you.

Greater Than a Tourist- Memphis Tennessee USA by Claude L Chafin offers the inside scoop on Memphis. Most travel books tell you how to travel like a tourist. Although there is nothing wrong with that, as part of the Greater Than a Tourist series, this book will give you travel tips from someone who has lived at your next travel destination.

In these pages, you will discover advice that will help you throughout your stay. This book will not tell you exact addresses or store hours but instead will give you excitement and knowledge from a local that you may not find in other smaller print travel books.

Travel like a local. Slow down, stay in one place, and get to know the people and the culture. By the time you finish this book, you will be eager and prepared to travel to your next destination.

TABLE OF CONTENTS

DEDICATION

This book is dedicated to the nearly one million people in the greater Memphis area, who, by their actions, interests, and dedication, have given the world two important descriptions of our city: "The Friendliest City in the South" and "The Most Generous City in America."

ABOUT THE AUTHOR

Claude L Chafin is an eighty-year-old retired businessman who has been a resident of Memphis, Tennessee, for the past fifty-six years. In his retirement, he has spent his time writing articles, technical papers, and has published three books: "Always Start With a Clean Kitchen," "The Messenger," and "A Matter of Time."

A Memphian since he was transferred here in 1962, Claude Chafin began his own construction company in 1967, sold the company in 2000, completed a five year management contract, and officially retired on December 31, 2004.

He has been active in the community for decades, having served on numerous Boards, including the Board of the Brooks Museum and the Rotary Club of Germantown, where he was President and District Governor. He has been an active member of Carnival Memphis since 1996, serving on their Board of Directors for three terms, was chosen President of Carnival Memphis in 2004, and King of Carnival in 2007. He is in his sixth term as Chairman of Children's Charities Selection Committee, an entity within Carnival Memphis that spends the entire year raising funds for the most needy children in the community.

He is married with five children, eight grandchildren, and one great-granddaughter. He and his wife have lived in the same home in east Memphis since they finished construction in 1981.

HOW TO USE THIS BOOK

The Greater Than a Tourist book series was written by someone who has lived in an area for over three months. The goal of this book is to help travelers either dream or experience different locations by providing opinions from a local. The author has made suggestions based on their own experiences. Please do your own research before traveling to the area in case the suggested places are unavailable.

FROM THE PUBLISHER

Traveling can be one of the most important parts of a person's life. The anticipation and memories that you have are some of the best. As a publisher of the Greater Than a Tourist book series, as well as the popular 50 Things to Know book series, we strive to help you learn about new places, spark your imagination, and inspire you. Wherever you are and whatever you do I wish you safe, fun, and inspiring travel.

Lisa Rusczyk Ed. D.
CZYK Publishing

OUR STORY

Traveling is a passion of the "Greater than a Tourist" series creator. Lisa studied abroad in college, and for their honeymoon Lisa and her husband toured Europe. During her travels to Malta, an older man tried to give her some advice based on his own experience living on the island since he was a young boy. She was not sure if she should talk to the stranger but was interested in his advice. When traveling to some places she was wary to talk to locals because she was afraid that they weren't being genuine. Through her travels, Lisa learned how much locals had to share with tourists. Lisa created the "Greater Than a Tourist" book series to help connect people with locals. A topic that locals are very passionate about sharing.

WELCOME TO
> TOURIST

INTRODUCTION

Memphis, Tennessee, is one of the most famous cities in the world, thanks to Elvis Presley, Martin Luther King, Memphis barbeque, Federal Express, and St. Jude Children's Hospital. The city has the distinction of being named: "The friendliest city in the south," and "The most generous city in America." It has also been correctly dubbed, "The Distribution Capital of The World," thanks to Federal Express and UPS, both of whom have major hubs here, the Memphis International Airport, and the Mississippi River barge traffic. It was once reported by the Wall Street Journal that if one shipped a FedEx package from uptown New York City to Wall Street in lower Manhattan, that package came through Memphis first. Other FedEx hubs have relieved some of that pressure but the Memphis hub still sorts, delivers, and re-ships over a million packages a night.

There are five distinct sub-sections of greater Memphis: Downtown, Mid-town, East Memphis, North Memphis, and South Memphis. Most all of the tourist activities will be found in a straight-line corridor, west-to-east, from downtown, through midtown, and into east Memphis. The tourist attractions in those three areas are unlike anything else you will find in the United States.

The geography of Memphis proper shows two distinct boundaries: The Mississippi River is our city limit on the west side, and the Mississippi state line is the city limit on the south side. We are literally hemmed into the southwestern corner of the long narrow state of Tennessee.

My tour will take you Downtown, through Midtown, into East Memphis, and beyond, to provide you with all the tools you will need to enjoy your stay: what to wear, where to stay, what to expect, what to see, and most importantly… to prepare you for the unexpected! Have fun!

1. GETTING HERE

Memphis has the advantage of being logistically superior to other cities in the United States, which is one of the reasons Federal Express started here. We have a world-class airport, serving every major city in the world. We are the second largest freight airport in the world, second only to Hong Kong. We sit at the intersection of three major interstates, connecting us directly to the east coast, the west coast, Canada, and Mexico. And we have the Mississippi River at our doorstep, with constant tour boats harboring weekly from New Orleans to the south, St. Louis and Cincinnati to the north. We are not hard to find.

2. HOW MUCH MONEY IS ENOUGH

No Confederate money accepted as you may have been told. But US currency graciously accepted. You will find Memphis to be moderately priced in comparison to cities our size. Our restaurant's range from hamburger and barbeque joints to elegant steak houses, with New Orleans flavored Cajun, and great seafood in between. The prices vary as well, but never will you leave a restaurant feeling that you were over charged. The prices are competitive simply because there are so many options in our city. Our national reputation is one of barbeque, but that is just the beginning of what is available here. Restaurants in and around Memphis are known all over the world. And we receive international visitors taking advantage of those restaurants on a daily basis. Most every restaurant will serve beer, wine, and hard liquor, even on Sunday. Tipping is expected, and the accepted norm is 20%. I will include numerous restaurants in this virtual tour, but because of space I will omit many more than I will cover. It may require more than one trip to experience all that is available in our wonderful city.

3. WHAT TO WEAR

The dress code in Memphis is as varied as the food we serve. If you were visiting a burger or barbeque joint (we have hundreds of both), you would be comfortable in jeans and collared shirts. The ladies will be wearing skirts, slacks, and appropriate tops. Men would be very uncomfortable in tank tops and flip-flops. Women are generally acceptable in most any attire that they would wear on a shopping spree. For our more elegant steak houses, although not required, men would be more comfortable in sport coats (tieless) and slacks. In some cases, sport coats and jeans are also acceptable. Women should dress accordingly.

4. WHEN IS THE BEST TIME TO VISIT

This is the easiest question to answer. USA Today and Traveler's Magazine voted Memphis as the "Best city in the world to visit during the month of May." Activities are rampant during the month of May including the "International Barbeque Contest" and "Music Fest" both of which lure thousands of tourists. It is also easy to suggest the worst time to visit…July and August, unless you are a fan of high temperatures. Football season is also a great time to visit, with any number of college football teams playing every weekend. The anniversary dates of Elvis' birth in January, and the anniversary of his death in August, are both very popular visitors' dates, especially with the international guests.

5. WHERE TO STAY

This is a much harder question then "when." The flagship hotel in downtown Memphis is "The Peabody Hotel" ("The Mississippi Delta begins in the lobby of The Peabody": William Faulkner.) Other up-scale downtown hotels include "The Madison Hotel" with great river views; "The Weston" across the street from our basketball arena, FedEx Forum; and "The Crowne Plaza" across the street from the convention center. In between there are numerous boutiques, and economy hotels, equally well located, and in some cases, less expensive. In East Memphis, "The Hilton" qualifies as the best up-scale hotel, with numerous economy and mid-ranged hotels nearby.

For the more adventuresome, "The Guest House at Graceland" is adjacent to Elvis Presley's estate, "Graceland," and is a five-star hotel, in Whitehaven, Tennessee, just south of downtown Memphis. Within the Bass Pro Pyramid, in the downtown area, is the Big Cypress Lodge, atop the Bass Pro signature store, with fantastic river views.

6. TRANSPORTATION

You will be disappointed in the mass-transit options in Memphis. Public transportation for the tourist industry is nearly non-existent. We have no subways, passenger trains within the city, or easy means of reaching the outskirts of town. In downtown Memphis we have convenient trolleys that crisscross the city but they do not extend to the suburbs, or even to mid-town. Tour buses are available for larger groups. There are a number of horse-drawn carriages available in the immediate downtown area, but trips to midtown or east Memphis would be limited to buses, cabs, or car services. Otherwise, a private or rental car would be your best option.

7. HOW LONG TO STAY

If you are spending an afternoon and evening in Memphis on your way to other locations, you would probably want to stay downtown, take in one of the numerous walking-distance sights, eat in one of the number of downtown restaurants, and get a good night's sleep. On the other hand, if you have dreamed of this trip forever, and you want to take in everything available, you will be totally entertained for a week or more. It just takes a little planning…and a car.

8. WHAT TO SEE

I will list the forty-three most popular places to go and things to see in Memphis, from the subtle to the sublime. No matter your interest, no matter your taste, you will find each a pleasant surprise, and as you leave town you will promise yourself…I am coming back!

I will start with:

9. MUD ISLAND

Terrible name…great visit! Take the tram to Mud Island, the western-most attraction in the city, featured boldly in Tom Cruise's picture "The Firm." Once on the island you can walk from Cairo, Illinois, through Memphis, and on to New Orleans, in a scale model of the Mississippi River, complete with a scale model of every city along the way. Then treat yourself to a light lunch at one of the restaurants, or a bit of libation at one of the outdoor bars. Catch a show in the amphitheater, or tour the Mud Island Museum with artifacts dating back to the nineteenth century.

10. BASS PRO AT THE PYRAMID

Visit Bass Pro's flagship shop in the iconic pyramid building, 120,000 square feet of shopping for all things outdoor and hunting. Take advantage of the sky-lift that elevates you to the very top of the pyramid for a panoramic view of the city, and three states, unavailable in any other venue in town. Enjoy a meal at one of the numerous restaurants, have a totty in the sky-bar, and if you get too tired by all there is to see, check into the Big Cypress Lodge for a great night's rest.

11. THE BEALE STREET LANDING

Stroll to the Mississippi River, descend to the river's edge, and watch an almost daily boat landing, filled with anxious and excited tourists like you. Watch a constant stream of riverboats and barges passing by while you sip a cold beer or a glass of wine. On your lucky day, a paddleboat will dock, and offer tours of their facilities, building an enthusiasm for a future trip down the Mississippi to New Orleans, maybe even for Mardi Gras!

]12. THE PEABODY HOTEL

Even if you are not staying there, the lobby of the Peabody is a "must see!" From the elaborate millwork, to the Peabody ducks, every view is a treat. The ducks are internationally famous. They reside on the Peabody roof and are marched into an elevator, then down to the lobby fountain at precisely 11:00 AM to the strands of "Stars and Stripes Forever" by John Phillip Sousa. They swim and flirt with the hotel guests for the day, and then they are marched back to the elevator and up to their rooftop quarters at precisely 5:00 PM. You might even follow them up to see where they live… the view from the Peabody roof deck is a show within itself. Very few visitors to Memphis will miss the opportunity to have a cocktail or two in the lobby of The Peabody. Every celebrity that visits the city will be seen in The Peabody lobby at least once during their visit. Southern Living Magazine ranks The Peabody Hotel as "The Best Hotel In The South."

13. BELZ MUSEUM OF ASIAN & JUDAIC ART

In 1998 the Belz family, owners of the Peabody Hotel, opened a small art museum featuring art from the Qing Dynasty, the last Dynasty of China dating to 1644-1911. Since then they have expanded the museum to 24,000 square feet with over 1,400 objects in their permanent collection. The museum is now informally referred to as the "Jade Museum" as the collection of jade artwork has become the most popular exhibit. Tourists are fascinated by the sheer size and detail of these ancient pieces. Some of the ornate horses and dragons are life size and the detail in each would tempt you to count the number of hairs in the horses mane, or the scales on the dragon's back. The museum is located just around the corner from the Peabody Hotel.

14. BEALE STREET

According to USA Today, Beale Street is the most popular street in America, beating out Bourbon Street. If you are a fan of people watching, street dancers, and music, this is the place for you! It is much like Bourbon Street only cleaner and louder.

For a special treat drop into A. Schwab's and have an old fashion ice cream soda at their soda bar. The doors and windows of every restaurant and bar are always open allowing those inside to experience the excitement and bustle of the crowds outside. B.B. King's offers constant music, from blues to soul. You might even be lucky enough to experience Billy Joel sitting in on an impromptu jam session. And for a real treat, sit on the patio of Silky O'Sullivan's and watch the goats pick up a beer and chug it! Warning: Do not leave your beer unattended! Plan on staying late. Beale Street doesn't warm up until at least nine o'clock and the bars are open until 3:00 AM.

15. THE NATIONAL CIVIL RIGHTS MUSEUM

This stop is one of the two most popular tourist attractions in the city, tracing the struggles of the black community back through the years, in the very location where Martin Luther King was assassinated…The Lorraine Motel. It is another of the "must see" locations in Memphis. The motel site has been expanded to include most every civil rights event that has occurred in the US in the last half century. Annual celebrations include the anniversary of Martin Luther King's assassination, and the pivotal "I am a man!" march that brought him here. It is open daily and is a four-block walk from The Peabody.

16. THE GREEN LINE RIVER BRIDGE WALK

A one and a half mile walk across the Mississippi River into the State of Arkansas, suspended on a cantilevered covered walkway attached to the old railroad bridge crossing the river. The sights from the middle of the bridge (and river) back toward Memphis are spectacular. Bikers and pedestrians share an enclosed walkway, suspended from the railroad crossing, attracting walkers and bicyclers from all across the nation to this very unique facility. Bring your cameras! The views of the city and barges passing underneath are a big hit. It is a very nice three-mile walk before lunch or before happy hour!

17. GRACELAND

The most iconic and popular attraction in Memphis, visited by nearly a million people every year, especially on his birthday… January 8th, and the anniversary of his death, August 16th. Whitehaven, the location of Graceland is just south of downtown and easy to get to. All of the original furniture, belongings, outfits, jewelry, instruments, are still there as they were when he died. The Lisa Marie, his private jet is parked across the street. Elvis is buried in the yard adjoining the estate as he requested in his will. The elaborate display of his many costumes is reason enough to make the visit if nothing else. The music note gates fronting the property have become the most popular photo op in the city. It is interesting to realize that Elvis Presley Enterprises is worth a lot more today than it was when he was alive, and it is said that he is equally as popular.

18. THE RENDEZVOUS

Almost as iconic as Graceland and The Peabody, this alley barbeque rib place is another of Memphis' "must visit" places. The Rendezvous has served every president since Ronald Reagan, The Beatles, Billy Joel, Elton John, and a list of others too long to print. It has also served most every citizen of Memphis on every occasion where there is guest in town to be entertained. But be aware, the waiters are extremely impatient. When they walk to your table (which they do very quickly) they want to hear you say, "half order" of "full order," and nothing more. Any hesitation, as if you are trying to decide what you want, you will hear, "I'll be right back." And you probably will never see them again. You go to the Rendezvous to have ribs! If you don't want ribs… go somewhere else.

19. GUS' WORLD FAMOUS FRIED CHICKEN

Even if The Rendezvous were not a world famous restaurant it would have made my list of "must see" places anyway because it is so much a part of Memphis lore. However, no list of Memphis places to see would be complete without including at least some of our famous eating establishments. Gus' World Famous Fried Chicken is one of those establishments. If you are a fan of spicy-hot chicken, this your place. It helps that one of their several locations in Memphis is located within walking distance of The Peabody. The "hot level" of Gus' chicken does not distract from the good taste of the chicken itself. The "hot level" of Gus' chicken is second only to Nashville's famous hot chicken place, Hattie B's, which lists it's hottest chicken as: "Shut The Cluck Up!"

20. LOFLIN YARD

One of the most unique restaurant/bars in the city, with two acres of outdoor seating, picnic tables, "corn hole" boards, ping pong tables, a water fall, a "safe house," and all round gathering place for visitors and locals alike. The local bands (of which there are many) provide live music both day and night. It is also within walking distance of The Peabody, in the heart of downtown Memphis. As a visiting tourist, you will enjoy watching a little of the eccentric side of Memphis locals. And while you are there, have one of their signature drinks, like the famous Hot Apple Cider & Bourbon.

21. OLD DOMINICK DISTILLERY

Originally established in 1843, this mainstay distillery was once the heart of early Memphis economy. It has been re-established into one of Memphis' most popular tourist stops. Visitors watch the process of bourbon making, and if interested, partake in some the product. But even for teetotalers, the tour is worth the stop. Located on Front Street, with views of the Mississippi River, it is a delightful alternative to conventional museums, where you will learn the history of Memphis from a more realistic approach. Memphis history in the nineteenth century was a wilder river town than even New Orleans. Old Dominick allows you that feeling.

22. CROSSTOWN CONCOURSE

No "must see" list would be complete without including this most unique property. It is not a stretch to suggest that there is nothing like it in the world. Originally Sears & Roebuck's largest distribution center, this 1.5 million square feet building has been transformed into a city. It is indeed a city within itself. Inside you will find: apartments, private

31

condos, restaurants, bars, art shops, a health facility, a high school, outdoor playgrounds, and numerous privately owned businesses much like a shopping mall. As the developers have said, you can be born there, raised there, go through high school there, and never leave the building. It is indeed a very unique facility. A stand-alone parking garage provides ample parking, which allows easy access in and out. Enjoy an ice cream cone in the morning and a stronger libation in the afternoon.

23. STAX MUSIC MUSEUM

Memphis is not only known for its barbeque, it is also known for its music. The heart of the Memphis music industry was Stax Records. Established in 1957, Stax Records literally changed the music world. No longer were big bands the most popular form of music. No longer was "Rock and Roll" the newest thing. Stax introduced the world to "soul music." Stax went bankrupt in 1975, a result of a distribution conflict with CBS Records. But the studio was reborn in 2003 when the facility became Stax Museum of American Soul Music. Now visitors will tour the studios that made hundreds of million-selling records,

by some of the best-known entertainers in the world:
Elvis Presley, Otis Redding, Sam & Dave, The Staple
Singers, Booker T & The MGs, Al Green, Rufus
Thomas, Aretha Franklin, Stevie Wonder, Marvin
Gaye, Sam Cooke, The Jackson Five. The list will
exceed the space I have, but it is a Memphis-Must-
See.

24. PAYNE'S BBQ

Tucked inside a 1950s style service station, just
outside the main east-west corridor of Memphis,
connecting downtown to east Memphis, resides
Payne's BBQ. The parking lot of this true Memphis
BBQ house is constantly full of out-of-state cars.
Payne's has been featured in several national cooking
shows and has therefore gained a considerable
following. It is a family run business, with all the
food prepared behind a counter in full view of the
buying public. Everyone behind the counter is family.
The BBQ is fantastic and the hot sauce is even better.
But if you are uncomfortable sitting in one of their
few straight-back chairs eating off of plastic
tablecloths, their take-out business is a popular
feature.

25. FLIGHT

While on the subject of food, for those not interested in hot chicken or barbeque, we have Flight, a downtown five-star restaurant, located on Main Street, one block from the Mississippi River. The restaurant features a full menu of steaks and seafood, and is the winner of Wine Spectator Magazine's Award of Excellence Award, as well as numerous James Beard awards. It is indeed a treat to sit on the outside covered patio on a fresh spring day and watch the trolley cars rumble by while you sip on your favorite chardonnay. The wait staff will remind you of the nicest restaurants in downtown New York City. Bring a credit card!

26. TROLLEYS

Of course we have trolleys! What great American city doesn't? Our trolleys, some of which were built in the early twentieth century, traverse the downtown area, connecting sites both north and south of downtown, as well as the medical center to the east. And while they do provide an excellent alternative to driving or walking, their main attraction is sightseeing. Tourists and locals will sit on wooden seats next to windows that are wide open and view our city from a prospective unavailable to autos or on foot. They are as much fun to watch as they are to ride, and you can hear them rumbling toward you from a block away… bells clanging all the way. Do not cross the street in front of them. They cannot stop!

27. AUTOZONE PARK

If you visit during baseball season, walk one block from The Peabody Hotel and enjoy a baseball game featuring the Memphis Redbirds, a farm club of the St. Louis Cardinals. And while most visitors to the games will admit that the draw may be the baseball team, but the real show is the stadium itself, voted the most beautiful baseball park in the south by Travel Magazine. And the food, unlike most ballparks, is delicious! The stadium is also home to numerous outdoor events including firework displays and touring bands, as well as the finish line of the annual St. Jude Marathon, which boasts over 30,000 runners a year. From street level on the outside it does not appear to be a baseball stadium. It almost looks like one of the buildings that surround it. Only the massive lights overhead, and the smell of their signature dish… cheese and BBQ nachos, gives it away.

28. THE ORPHEUM THEATER

Home to every Broadway traveling show, the Orpheum Theater is a crown jewel on its own. The building was completed in 1890 as the Grand Opera House, filled with artisan millwork, a massive center-stairway, and ornate décor unavailable in today's construction. It became the Orpheum Theater in 1928, was remodeled in the late 1980s and seats 2860 for most Broadway shows. It is located on Main Street just south of downtown, at the foot of Beale Street. There is ample parking in the lot that adjoins, and the trolleys pass the front door on a regular basis.

29. OVERTON SQUARE

Just east of the downtown area, encompassing sixteen square blocks sits a local haven for boutiques, restaurants, and street art shows, named Overton Square. It is the home of The Memphis Ballet Company, Circuit Playhouse, Hattiloo Theater, Malco Studio on the Square, and Playhouse on the Square, all designed for stage productions. It is also the home of Lafayette's Music Room, a popular bar and restaurant where an unknown Billy Joel made one of his first appearances. And if you are in the mood for a great burger, while sitting on the patio, try Belly Acres "Farm to Table Burgers!" Of course libations are available day and night!

30. RHODES COLLEGE

A private liberal arts college, Rhodes sits on 123-acres and boasts of over 2,000 students. A walking tour of the campus is inspiring. The Princeton Review named Rhodes "The #1 Most Beautiful College Campus in America." Newsweek named it "America's #1 Service-Oriented College." Every building on campus features stone gothic architecture, surrounded by over 1500 century old trees. It is important and impressive that the college can boast of a 10 to I student to teacher ratio, but a visitor will be equally impressed by sitting on a freshly mowed lawn, or one of the numerous park benches, and watching the future of America walking by.

31. THE MEMPHIS ZOO

Like Panda Bears? We have several at the zoo, including a newborn, offspring of Ya Ya and Le Le. The Memphis Zoo was opened in 1906, encompasses 76 acres, and has over 3500 animals representing over 500 species in residence. In 2008 TripAdvisor Magazine ranked the Memphis Zoo "#1 Zoo in America." Since 1990, more than $100 million has been spent on renovations and expansions. Today the zoo's animals reside in three zones: Teton Trek, Northwest Passage, and China. The zoo also prides itself on a magnificent lodge, used for private occasions, and several restaurants. It is a fun way to entertain the young ones for an afternoon, especially feeding the giraffes from a raised platform. The giraffes extend their tongues a full one-foot outside their mouths to surround every morsel offered them. Most youngsters panic and drop the morel before the tongue gets close but the giraffe will wait patiently until it is offered a second time.

32. BROOKS MUSEUM OF ART

After your visit to the Memphis Zoo, reward yourself with a stop in the zoo's front yard at the

Brooks Museum of Art. Completed in 1916, Brooks Museum of Art is a registered U.S. National Landmark. The Beaux-Arts building was designed by James Gamble Rogers and donated to the city by Bessie Vance Brooks in memory of her husband. There are 29 galleries and art classrooms and over 4500 works of art in the permanent collection. Lunch and cocktails are served in the dining room for those exhausted from the tours of permanent or traveling exhibits. The setting is park-like and inviting, the staff helpful, and the exhibits first class.

33. SUN STUDIO

Sun Studio, home of Sun Records since the early 1960s, can boast of one of the most iconic events in "rock and roll" music, an event that inspired a movie and a television series. The famed Sun Studio "Million Dollar Quartet": Elvis Presley, Johnny Cash, Jerry Lee Lewis, and Roy Orbison, sitting in an impromptu jam session that made rock and roll what it is today. The tours of this studio are indeed inspiring and historic. Where else can you hold the microphone that Elvis Presley sang into? Where else can you sit in the same studio where Johnny Cash recorded "Daddy Sang Bass"? This is an active studio where U2 has recorded, as have Tom Petty, Paul Simon, and Matchbox 20. There are daily tours, and it is located just east of downtown Memphis.

34. HARBOR TOWN

Before we leave the downtown area, you must be introduced to Harbor Town. If there is one place in Memphis that would convince you to move here it is Harbor Town. Located as far west as one can go and still be in Tennessee, Harbor Town is a most cosmopolitan address. Magnificent homes and condos sit right at the waters edge. The only thing separating these homes and the river is a walking park that is one mile long. There are wonderful restaurants: Miss Cordelia's Table, Paulette's, Café Eclectic, Terrace at the River Inn, and Tugs. There is but one hotel: The River Inn at Harbor Town. There is one grocery store: Miss Cordelia's Grocery. The views are spectacular, and the feeling is posh! The river boats float less than a football field away, splashing water in every direction as if saying, "Get out of my way!" It is a sight you will not see anywhere else.

35. ERNESTINE & HAZEL'S

I probably should have listed this place closer to the top so you wouldn't miss it. But alas, it will stay here. Ernestine & Hazel's was at one time, in Memphis' early days... a brothel. Tales from the past tell of riverboats stopping on the bank just below this establishment allowing the passengers to disembark for a quick visit to the brothel. Hours later the boat crews would be sent to round everyone up and drag them back to the boats. Today it is an eccentric place to be seen. The greasy burgers and fries are to die for. This corner bar will seat a dozen people comfortably, yet as many as fifty or sixty can be in the bar at one time. A side trip to the very small rooms upstairs is a must. One has to wonder why those rooms are so small. Today's tourists require much more space than those rooms provide. Makes one wonder how they stayed in business.

36. CENTRAL BBQ

Back to food again! And why not, we are in Memphis!! This establishment wins "best of" more than its share of the time and with little wonder. Sitting outside on an elevated patio, eating some of

41

Memphis' best barbeque, beans, and slaw, while being entertained by a happy and riotous crowd, is worth the price. What's not to like. The location is perfect for the city, away from downtown, yet not confused with other east Memphis BBQ joints, on the edge of the eccentric Cooper-Young district. Sit on that patio long enough and you will see more than one or two well known Memphis visitors who have been directed to that patio by well-informed Memphians.

37. COOPER-YOUNG

And speaking of Cooper-Young, a tourist map of Memphis would be incomplete without directions to this thriving community. Sitting amidst a neighborhood of 1900-era homes, you will find a repository of restaurants, bars, bookstores, art shops, and sidewalks full of people. One gains access to the area by passing under a railroad crossing adorned on the side with artwork: a full rendering of those 1900-era homes, standing side-by-side as if to say, "Welcome home!" While there, be sure to drop in Burke's Book Store for an amazing collection of new and collectable books. And for a taste of Charleston,

South Carolina, have a snack, full meal, or a glass of
wine, at Sweet Grass. It is worth the visit.

38. SOUL FISH CAFÉ

Of the numerous Cooper-Young eating
establishments you will be tempted to visit, one
serves the best catfish and trimmings to be found
outside of Mississippi or Louisiana: Soul Fish Café.
So after an hour or so of visiting all the shops in the
area, it might be necessary to stop at the counter of
Soul Fish Café and ask for a "to go" order of fish and
fries, then reward yourself by indulging in this sinful
dish as you make your way to your next Memphis
sight. Unfortunately, no beer to go!

39. CHILDREN'S MUSEUM

We must leave food for a moment (which is hard
to do in Memphis) to tour another of Memphis'
jewels: The Children's Museum. Your young ones
will be greatly entertained by a full range of "hands
on" activities that will stimulate their imaginations.
They can fish for wooden fish in a long streaming
canal. They can steer a relic fire engine wearing an

43

authentic fireman's helmet, build wooden blocks to exaggerated heights, or experiment with airflow through the largest airflow tubes in the world. And best of all, ride the newly remodeled carrousel that once captured every child's fantasy when it was in full operation at the Memphis Fairgrounds.

40. THE PINK PALACE

This pink Georgian marble structure was originally the private home of Clarence Saunders, the founder of the Piggly Wiggly chain of grocery stores. The building was built in 1923, is in excess of 25,000 square feet and sits on a piece of property large enough for an eighteen-hole golf course. Today it houses a Planetarium, an IMAX theater, a natural history museum, and is visited by 250,000 people a year. One of the exhibits is a complete replica of the original Piggly Wiggly store, the first "self service" grocery store in America. Patrons would enter the store on one side, push a cart in one direction down aisle after aisle until they came to the final aisle where they would find a "check out" employee and pay for all the goods they had picked up. Before that concept people would walk to a grocery store counter, tell the employee what they wanted, and he would go get the item and bring it back to the customer. Can you imagine going through that process today?

41. BROTHER JUNIPER'S

What? You thought I was through with food? Unique is the only word for this breakfast establishment. It has won the "Best Breakfast in Memphis" award so many times they are thinking of retiring the award. Rachel Ray, of television fame says it even better. She calls it the "Best Breakfast in the Nation!" They are known for their fresh-baked artisan bread, cooked in an apprenticeship program, on site, by "at-risk" youth. Located on the outskirts of The University of Memphis, this should be the first stop of the day for knowledgeable travelers, before beginning my list of Memphis places to see. You will need the energy!

42. MEMPHIS BOTANIC GARDENS

Just a short drive from Brother Juniper's you will want to visit the Botanic Gardens, nature's gift to Memphis. Inside you will find enough diversion to keep an entire family interested. The Japanese Garden, the Asian Garden, and the Herb Garden will fascinate the adults. And "My Big Back Yard" will keep the children interested and busy for hours. They can climb to the tree house and descend through a fully enclosed, twisty slide. They can crawl through earthen "mole holes" lined with 36" culverts. They can visit small structures that look like homes for elves. There are slides, waterfalls, sand piles, and even a scheduled thunderstorm. It is indeed a child's heaven.

43. DIXON GALLERIES AND GARDENS

Mere steps from the front door of the Botanic Garden you will find the Dixon Galleries. Built on seventeen acres beneath tall oak and poplar trees, the Dixon Galleries, originally a private home built in 1923, entertains more than a half million visitors a year. Their permanent collection includes French and American impressionist works, as well as the Stout Collection of 18th Century porcelain. The expansive lawn in the back, surrounded one-hundred-year old trees and gardens is the perfect venue for early evening concerts by the Memphis Symphony Orchestra. What a delight to bring a blanket, a cooler full of your favorite wine, your picnic basket filled with delicacies, and maybe a candelabra for effect, while you listen to string music. It is just another of Memphis' crown jewels.

44. GALLOWAY GOLF COURSE

Most every city of our size has its fair share of public golf courses. Memphis has nine. But the Galloway Golf Course is a little different. Situated in the midst of an upscale east Memphis neighborhood, this par 70 golf course features tall trees, rolling fairways, terraced greens, and deep sand traps. It is as close to a private, manicured, golf course you will find. The clubhouse offers nourishing snacks and post-round libations to settle the frayed nerves. For those golf enthusiasts, an early more round of golf before continuing our tour of places to see and things to do in Memphis is a nice beginning.

45. SHELBY FARMS PARK

If you are not from Memphis you probably didn't realize that we have a public park larger than New York's Central Park. It is, in fact, five times larger! At 4,500 acres, Shelby Farms Park is one of the largest public parks in the country. Situated on the eastern-most edge of Memphis city limits, the park is a haven for bike enthusiasts, runners, fishermen, walkers, boaters, and treetop climbers. For bicyclists, the Shelby Farms Greenline presents 6.5 miles of uninterrupted paved surface. For fishermen, a near 50 acre stocked lake provides plenty of opportunities for bragging rights. And where else in the world, short of Montana, can one see a herd of Buffalo! Shelby Farms boasts 50 acres of pasture reserved for these magnificent creatures. When the children are not captivated by the Buffalo, they are drawn to the Woodland Discovery Playground, which is much more than simply a playground. Certified by the Sustainable Sites Initiative, the playground provides a creative learning experience like none other.

46. THE KITCHEN AT SHELBY FARMS

Reservations are required. Ah, but it is worth it. The Kitchen, is a restaurant that stands beside the fifty-acre lake at Shelby Farms, and features both indoor and outdoor seating. To dine while looking into an evening sunset, the ever-changing colors reflecting off of the water, is an experience like none other. And I haven't even mentioned the food. The chefs are some of the best known in the city. The menu is as varied as the activities around you, and their extensive wine cellars provide a wide range of American, French, Australian, and Italian wines. Most of the fresh produce is grown on the numerous gardens that occupy large swaths of the farm around the facility. Knowledgeable Memphis residents treat their out-of-town guests at The Kitchen on their first evening in town, as a way of showing off our favorite city. The guests are always impressed. Might as well start things off on the right foot.

47. THE FARMER'S MARKET AT SHELBY FARMS

Few experiences in life are as invigorating as strolling through the aisles of fresh produce at The Farmer's Market at Shelby Farms on a crisp Saturday morning. The aromas are intoxicating. From the delightfully sweet smell of fresh strawberries to eye-watering piquant smell of yellow onions, every farmer's booth provides a new temptation. Memphians are known to do a week's worth of produce shopping on those Saturday mornings, knowing full well they are buying more than they can possibly eat in a week. Better to be prepared than to run out mid-week and no place else to go for the fresh stuff. Wal-Mart can't touch the freshness of The Farmer's Market!

48. THE LICHTERMAN NATURE CENTER

The Lichterman Nature Center, a division of The Pink Palace Family of Museums is a 65-acre native wildlife habitat, featuring three miles of walking trails through dense trees and undergrowth. It is the home to numerous native plants, birds, mammals, and amphibians, all within eyesight and touch. The Nature Center provides a "hands-on" environmental experience, including microscopic details and under water viewing, with specialized programs exploring the three distinct habitats at the center: lake, meadow, and forest. As an added bonus, the fall season offers an extensive plant sale and privet pulls.

49. GERMANTOWN

All of the tourist locations on this tour to this point have been within the city limits of Memphis. But our tourist attractions are not limited to those within the city limits. Many wonderful tourist stops are located outside of the city. Germantown is one of those stops. Germantown is a "bedroom community" on the eastern border of Memphis. But for the city limit signs one would never know when they had crossed from Memphis to Germantown. The city of Germantown continues to grow at a rapid rate, but the "old town" maintains its early America appeal. The vacated train depot is constantly maintained as one of the numerous symbols of this very proud neighborhood, known extensively for the horse business. There is, in fact, a speed limit for horses (10

51

miles per hour) posted alongside the auto speed limit. The Germantown Charity Horse Show is a nationally known affair, attracting horses from all over the world. This tour will highlight several of the more popular establishments of this quaint little town.

50. THE COMMISSARY

Not to be outdone by the Memphis barbeque reputation, The Commissary in Germantown offers a BBQ spread surpassed by none. Legend has their BBQ beginnings traced to a small outdoor grill. They used that grill for smoking pork sandwiches for the lunch crowd that arrived daily to what was at the time a quaint little grocery store. They don't sell groceries anymore. The large dinner crowd will squeeze into the small, red and white checkered tablecloth-covered tables, taking up every square inch of the space. Benches on the outside front porch accommodate the awaiting crowd, sometimes exceeding dozens. A hostess will take your name, then call you when it is your turn to wind your way through the mass of humanity, on your way to a prized possession: a table. It is entirely worth the wait.

BONUS. SOUTHERN SOCIAL

Just down the street from The Commissary, in "old town" Germantown, in case you are not interested in barbeque, sits a true American food restaurant known as Southern Social. The setting is in one of Germantown's original structures alongside the Southern Railway tracks. The food would remind you of the meals your mother or grandmother used to make, from deviled eggs and fried pimento cheese sandwiches to Beef Wellington. Relax in the large bar and people watch. Southern Social is a delightful way to spend the evening, restaurant or otherwise.

There you have it, fifty-one tips for travel to Memphis, Tennessee, USA. But I could not include everything. I probably left out the best parts. If you make the journey to our wonderful city you might leave saying, "Well I wonder why he didn't mention this?" I apologize in advance for all oversights. And even though I have given you fifty-one tips on visiting our city, I offer a few reasons why you should:

Southerners like those of us living in Memphis have a reputation. And some of it is not so good. But some of it is also not deserved. So the first

53

reason I think you should visit is to meet the people who live here. They are generous, helpful, considerate, hard working, and family oriented. National companies like Federal Express, AutoZone, International Paper, St. Jude, ServiceMaster, Mueller Industries, and numerous others, came to look at us and decided to stay. You might too.

The natural resources surrounding our city are not to be missed. The Mississippi River is one of the most dominant features of the United States, sending a billion gallons of water to the Gulf of Mexico every minute. Our landscape is as flat as a tabletop allowing multistate views from almost any elevation. Farmland is abundant and provides scenic views of rich crops in almost every direction.

And finally, the city itself, the people, the businesses, the churches, the entertainment, the laughter that fills the air no matter where you go. Memphis is an active town, thriving on the ambitions of a million people, each one wanting the best for their families and the community. We would love to entertain you.

BONUS BOOK

50 THINGS TO KNOW ABOUT PACKING LIGHT FOR TRAVEL

PACK THE RIGHT WAY EVERY TIME

AUTHOR: MANIDIPA BHATTACHARYYA

Edited by Melanie Howthorne

ABOUT THE AUTHOR

Manidipa Bhattacharyya is a creative writer and editor, with an
education in English literature and Linguistics. After working in the IT
industry for seven long years she decided to call it quits and follow her
heart instead. Manidipa has been ghost writing, editing, proof reading
and doing secondary research services for many story tellers and article
writers for about three years. She stays in Kolkata, India with her
husband and a busy two year old. In her own time Manidipa enjoys
travelling, photography and writing flash fiction.

Manidipa believes in travelling light and never carries anything that she
couldn't haul herself on a trip. However, travelling with her child
changed the scenario. She seemed to carry the entire world with her for
the baby on the first two trips. But good sense prevailed and she is
again working her way to becoming a light traveler, this time with a
kid.

INTRODUCTION

He who would travel happily
must travel light.

-Antoine de Saint-Exupéry

Travel takes you to different places from seas and mountains to deserts and much more. In your travels you get to interact with different people and their cultures. You will, however, enjoy the sights and interact positively with these new people even more, if you are travelling light.

When you travel light your mind can be free from worry about your belongings. You do not have to spend precious vacation time waiting for your luggage to arrive after a long flight. There is be no chance of your bags going missing and the best part is that you need not pay a fee for checked baggage.

People who have mastered this art of packing light will root for you to take only one carry-on, wherever you go. However, many people can find it really hard to pack light. More so if you are travelling with children. Differentiating between "must have" and "just in case" items is the starting point. There will be ample shopping avenues at your destination which are just waiting to be explored.

This book will show you 'packing' in a new 'light' – pun intended – and help you to embrace light packing practices for all of your future travels.

Off to packing!

DEDICATION

I dedicate this book to all the travel buffs that I know, who have given me great insights into the contents of their backpacks.

THE RIGHT TRAVEL GEAR

1. CHOOSE YOUR TRAVEL GEAR CAREFULLY

While selecting your travel gear, pick items that are light weight, durable and most importantly, easy to carry. There are cases with wheels so you can drag them along – these are usually on the heavy side because of the trolley. Alternatively a backpack that you can carry comfortably on your back, or even a duffel bag that you can carry easily by hand or sling across your body are also great options. Whatever you choose, one thing to keep in mind is that the luggage itself should not weigh a ton, this will give you the flexibility to bring along one extra pair of shoes if you so desire.

2. CARRY THE MINIMUM NUMBER OF BAGS

Selecting light weight luggage is not everything. You need to restrict the number of bags you carry as well. One carry-on size bag is ideal for light travel. Most carriers allow one cabin baggage plus one purse, handbag or camera bag as long as it slides under the seat in front. So technically, you can carry two items of luggage without checking them in.

3. PACK ONE EXTRA BAG

Always pack one extra empty bag along with your essential items. This could be a very light weight duffel bag or even a sturdy tote bag which takes up minimal space. In the event that you end up buying a lot of souvenirs, you already have a handy bag to stuff all that into and do not have to spend time hunting for an appropriate bag.

I'm very strict with my packing and have everything in its right place. I never change a rule. I hardly use anything in the hotel room. I wheel my own wardrobe in and that's it.

Charlie Watts

CLOTHES & ACCESSORIES

4. PLAN AHEAD

Figure out in advance what you plan to do on your trip. That will help you to pick that one dress you need for the occasion. If you are going to attend a wedding then you have to carry formal wear. If not, you can ditch the gown for something lighter that will be comfortable during long walks or on the beach.

5. WEAR THAT JACKET

Remember that wearing items will not add extra luggage for your air travel. So wear that bulky jacket that you plan to carry for your trip. This saves space and can also help keep you warm during the chilly flight.

6. MIX AND MATCH

Carry clothes that can be interchangeably used to reinvent your look. Find one top that goes well with a couple of pairs of pants or skirts. Use tops, shirts and jackets wisely along with other accessories like a scarf or a stole to create a new look.

7. CHOOSE YOUR FABRIC WISELY

Stuffing clothes in cramped bags definitely takes its toll which results in wrinkles. It is best to carry wrinkle free, synthetic clothes or merino tops. This will eliminate the need for that small iron you usually bring along.

8. DITCH CLOTHES PACK UNDERWEAR

Pack more underwear and socks. These are the things that will give you a fresh feel even if you do not get a chance to wear fresh clothes. Moreover these are easy to wash and can be dried inside the hotel room itself.

9. CHOOSE DARK OVER LIGHT

While picking your clothes choose dark coloured ones. They are easy to colour coordinate and can last longer before needing a wash. Accidental food spills and dirt from the road are less visible on darker clothes.

10. WEAR YOUR JEANS

Take only one pair of Jeans with you, which you should wear on the flight. Remember to pick a pair that can be worn for sightseeing trips and is equally eloquent for dinner. You can add variety by adding light weight cargoes and chinos.

11. CARRY SMART ACCESSORIES

The right accessory can give you a fresh look even with the same old dress. An intelligent neck-piece, a couple of bright scarves, stoles or a sarong can be used in a number of ways to add variety to your clothing. These light weight beauties can double up as a nursing cover, a light blanket, beach wear, a modesty cover for visiting places of worship, and also makes for an enthralling game of peek-a-boo.

12. LEARN TO FOLD YOUR GARMENTS

Seasoned travellers all swear by rolling their clothes for compact and wrinkle free packing. Bundle packing, where you roll the clothes around a central object as if tying it up, is also a popular method of compact and wrinkle free packing. Stacking folded clothes one on top of another is a big no-no as it makes creases extreme and they are difficult to get rid of without ironing.

13. WASH YOUR DIRTY LAUNDRY

One of the ways to avoid carrying loads of clothes is to wash the clothes you carry. At some places you might get to use the laundry services or a Laundromat but if you are in a pinch, best solution is to wash them yourself. If that is the plan then carrying quick drying clothes is highly recommended, which most often also happen to be the wrinkle free variety.

14. LEAVE THOSE TOWELS BEHIND

Regular towels take up a lot of space, are heavy and take ages to dry out. If you are staying at hotels they will provide you with towels anyway. If you are travelling to a remote place, where the availability of towels look doubtful, carry a light weight travel towel of viscose material to do the job.

15. USE A COMPRESSION BAG

Compression bags are getting lots of recommendation now days from regular travellers. These are useful for saving space in your luggage when you have to pack bulky dresses. While packing for the return trip, get help from the hotel staff to arrange a vacuum cleaner.

FOOTWEAR

16. PUT ON YOUR HIKING BOOTS

If you have plans to go hiking or trekking during your trip, you will need those bulky hiking boots. The best way to carry them is to wear them on flight to save space and luggage weight. You can remove the boots once inside and be comfortable in your socks.

17. PICKING THE RIGHT SHOES

Shoes are often the bulkiest items, along with being the dainty if you are a female. They need care and take up a lot of space in your luggage. It is advisable therefore to pick shoes very carefully. If you plan to do a lot of walking and site seeing, then wearing a pair of comfortable walking shoes are a must. For more formal occasions you can carry durable, light weight flats which will not take up much space.

18. STUFF SHOES

If you happen to pack a pair of shoes, ensure you utilize their hollow insides. Tuck small items like rolled up socks or belts to save space. They will also be easy to find.

TOILETRIES

19. STASHING TOILETRIES

Carry only absolute necessities. Airline rules dictate that for one carry-on bag, liquids and gels must be in 3.4 ounce (100ml) bottles or less, and must be packed in a one quart zip-lock bag. If you are planning to stay in a hotel, the basic things will be provided for you. It's best is to buy the rest from the local market at your destination.

20. TAKE ALONG TAMPONS

Tampons are a hard to find item in a lot of countries. Figure out how many you need and pack accordingly. For longer stays you can buy them online and have them delivered to where you are staying.

21. GET PAMPERED BEFORE YOU TRAVEL

Some avid travellers suggest getting a pedicure and manicure just the day before travelling. This not only gives you a well kept look, you also save the trouble of packing nail polish. Remember, every little bit of weight reduced adds up.

ELECTRONICS
22. LUGGING ALONG ELECTRONICS

Electronics have a large role to play in our lives today. Most of us cannot imagine our lives away from our phones, laptops or tablets. However while travelling, one must consider the amount of weight these electronics add to our luggage. Thankfully smart phones come along with all the essentials tools like a camera, email access, picture editing tools and more. They are smart to the point of eliminating the need to carry multiple gadgets. Choose a smart phone that suits all your requirements and travel with the world in your palms or pocket.

23. REDUCE THE NUMBER OF CHARGERS

If you do travel with multiple electronic devices, you will have to bear the additional burden of carrying all their chargers too. Check if a single charger can be used for multiple devices. You might also consider investing in a pocket charger. These small devices support multiple devices while keeping you charged on the go.

24. TRAVEL FRIENDLY APPS

Along with smart phones come numerous apps, which are immensely helpful in our travels. You name it and you have an app for it at hand – take pictures, sharing with friends and family, torch to light dark roads, maps, checking flight/train times, find hotels and many other things. Use these smart alternatives to traditional items like books to eliminate weight and save space.

I get ideas about what's essential when packing my suitcase.

-Diane von Furstenberg

TRAVELLING WITH KIDS

25. BRING ALONG THE STROLLER

Kids might enjoy walking for a while but they soon tire out and a stroller is the just the right thing for them to rest in while you continue your tour. Strollers also double duty as a luggage carrier and shopping bag holder. Remember to pick a light weight, easy to handle brand of stroller. Better yet, find out in advance if you can rent a stroller at your destination.

26. BRING ONLY ENOUGH DIAPERS FOR YOUR TRIP

Diapers take up a lot of space and add to the weight of your luggage. Therefore it is advisable to carry just enough diapers to last through the trip and a few for afterwards, till you buy fresh stock at your destination. Unless of course you are travelling to a really remote area, in which case you have no choice but to carry the load. Otherwise diapers are something you will find pretty easily.

27. TAKE ONLY A COUPLE OF TOYS

Children are easily attracted by new things in their environment. While travelling they will find numerous 'new' objects to scrutinize and play with. Packing just one favorite toy is enough, or if there is no favorite toy leave out all of them in favor of stories or imaginary games.

28. CARRY KID FRIENDLY SNACKS

Create a small snack counter in your bag to store away quick bites for those sudden hunger pangs. Depending on the child's age this could include chocolates, raisins, dry fruits, granola bars or biscuits. Also keep a bottle of water handy for your little one.

These things do not add much weight and can be adjusted in a handbag or knapsack.

29. GAMES TO CARRY

Create some travel specific, imaginary games if you have slightly grown up children, like spot the attractions. Keep a coloring book and colors handy for in-flight or hotel time. Apps on your smart phone can keep the children engaged with cartoons and story books. Older children are often entertained by games available on phones or tablets. This cuts the weight of luggage down while keeping the kids entertained.

30. LET THE KIDS CARRY THEIR LOAD

A good thing is to start early sharing of responsibilities. Let your child pick a bag of his or her choice and pack it themselves. Keep tabs on what they are stuffing in their bags by asking if they will be using that item on the trip. It could start out being just an entertainment bag initially but with growing years they will learn to sort the useful from the superfluous. Children as little as four can maneuver a small trolley suitcase like a pro- their experience in pull along toys credit. If you are worried that you may be pulling it for them, you may want to start with a backpack.

31. DECIDE ON LOCATION FOR CHILDREN TO SLEEP

While on a trip you might not always get a crib at your destination, and carrying one will make life all the more difficult. Instead call ahead to see if there are any cribs or roll out beds for children. You may even put blankets on the floor. Weave them a story about camping and they will gladly sleep without any trouble.

32. GET BABY PRODUCTS DELIVERED AT YOUR DESTINATION

If you are absolutely paranoid about not getting your favourite variety of diaper or brand of baby food, check out online stores like amazon.com for services in your destination city. You can buy things online ahead of your travel and get them delivered to your hotel upon arrival.

33. FEEDING NEEDS OF YOUR INFANTS

If you are travelling with a breastfed infant, you save the trouble of carrying bottles and bottle sanitization kits. For special food, or medications, you may need to call ahead to make sure you have a refrigerator where you are staying.

34. FEEDING NEEDS OF YOUR TODDLER

With the progression from infancy to toddler, their dietary requirements too evolve. You will have to pack some snacks for travelling time. Fresh fruits and vegetables can be purchased at your destination. Most of the cities you travel to in whichever part of the world, will have baby food products and formulas, available at the local drug-store or the supermarket.

35. PICKING CLOTHES FOR YOUR BABY

Contrary to popular belief, babies can do without many changes of clothes. At the most pack 2 outfits per day. Pack mix and match type clothes for your little one as well. Pick things which are comfortable to wear and quick to dry.

36. SELECTING SHOES FOR YOUR BABY

Like outfits, kids can make do with two pairs of comfortable shoes. If you can get some water resistant shoes it will be best. To expedite drying wet shoes, you can stuff newspaper in them then wrap

them with newspaper and leave them to dry
overnight.

37. KEEP ONE CHANGE OF CLOTHES HANDY

Travelling with kids can be tricky. Keep a change of
clothes for the kids and mum handy in your purse or
tote bag. This takes a bit of space in your hand
luggage but comes extremely handy in case there are
any accidents or spills.

38. LEAVE BEHIND BABY ACCESSORIES

Baby accessories like their bed, bath tub, car seat, crib
etc. should be left at home. Many hotels provide a
crib on request, while car seats can be borrowed from
friends or rented. Babies can be given a bath in the
hotel sink or even in the adult bath tub with a little bit
of water. If you bring a few bath toys, they can be
used in the bath, pool, and out of water. They can also
be sanitized easily in the sink.

39. CARRY A SMALL LOAD OF PLASTIC BAGS

With children around there are chances of a number
of soiled clothes and diapers. These plastic bags help
to sort the dirt from the clean inside your big bag.

These are very light weight and come in handy to other carry stuff as well at times.

PACK WITH A PURPOSE

40. PACKING FOR BUSINESS TRIPS

One neutral-colored suit should suffice. It can be paired with different shirts, ties and accessories for different occasions. One pair of black suit pants could be worn with a matching jacket for the office or with a snazzy top for dinner.

41. PACKING FOR A CRUISE

Most cruises have formal dinners, and that formal dress usually takes up a lot of space. However you might find a tuxedo to rent. For women, a short black dress with multiple accessory options will do the trick.

42. PACKING FOR A LONG TRIP OVER DIFFERENT CLIMATES

The secret packing mantra for travel over multiple climates is layering. Layering traps air around your body creating insulation against the cold. The same light t-shirt that is comfortable in a warmer climate can be the innermost layer in a colder climate.

REDUCE SOME MORE WEIGHT

43. LEAVE PRECIOUS THINGS AT HOME

Things that you would hate to lose or get damaged leave them at home. Precious jewelry, expensive gadgets or dresses, could be anything. You will not require these on your trip. Leave them at home and spare the load on your mind.

44. SEND SOUVENIRS BY MAIL

If you have spent all your money on purchasing souvenirs, carrying them back in the same bag that you brought along would be difficult. Either pack everything in another bag and check it in the airport or get everything shipped to your home. Use an international carrier for a secure transit, but this could be more expensive than the checking fees at the airport.

45. AVOID CARRYING BOOKS

Books equal to weight. There are many reading apps which you can download on your smart phone or tab.

Plus there are gadgets like Kindle and Nook that are thinner and lighter alternatives to your regular book.

CHECK, GET, SET, CHECK AGAIN

46. STRATEGIZE BEFORE PACKING

Create a travel list and prepare all that you think you need to carry along. Keep everything on your bed or floor before packing and then think through once again – do I really need that? Any item that meets this question can be avoided. Remove whatever you don't really need and pack the rest.

47. TEST YOUR LUGGAGE

Once you have fully packed for the trip take a test trip with your luggage. Take your bags and go to town for window shopping for an hour. If you enjoy your hour long trip it is good to go, if not, go home and reduce the load some more. Repeat this test till you hit the right weight.

48. ADD A ROLL OF DUCT TAPE

You might wonder why, when this book has been talking about reducing stuff, we're suddenly asking you to pack something totally unusual. This is because when you have limited supplies, duct tape is immensely helpful for small repairs – a broken bag, leaking zip-lock bag, broken sunglasses, you name it and duct tape can fix it, temporarily.

49. LIST OF ESSENTIAL ITEMS

Even though the emphasis is on packing light, there are things which have to be carried for any trip. Here is our list of essentials:

• Passport/Visa or any other ID

• Any other paper work that might be required on a trip like permits, hotel reservation confirmations etc.

• Medicines – all your prescription medicines and emergency kit, especially if you are travelling with children

• Medical or vaccination records

• Money in foreign currency if travelling to a different country

• Tickets- Email or Message them to your phone

50. MAKE THE MOST OF YOUR TRIP

Wherever you are going, whatever you hope to do we encourage you to embrace it whole-heartedly. Take in the scenery, the culture and above all, enjoy your time away from home.

On a long journey even a straw weighs heavy.

-Spanish Proverb

PACKING AND PLANNING TIPS

A Week before Leaving

- Arrange for someone to take care of pets and water plants

- Stop mail and newspaper

- Notify Credit Card companies where you are going.

- Change your thermostat settings

- Car inspected, oil is changed, and tires have the correct pressure.

- Passports and id is up to date.

- Pay bills.

- Copy important items and download travel Apps.

- Start collecting small bills for tips

Right Before Leaving

- Clean out refrigerator.

- Empty garbage cans.

- Lock windows.

- Make sure you have the right ID with you.

- Bring cash for tips.

- Remember travel documents.

- Lock door behind you.

- Remember wallet.

- Unplug items in house and pack chargers.

READ OTHER
GREATER THAN A TOURIST
BOOKS

Greater Than a Tourist San Miguel de Allende Guanajuato Mexico:
50 Travel Tips from a Local by Tom Peterson

Greater Than a Tourist – Lake George Area New York USA:
50 Travel Tips from a Local by Janine Hirschklau

Greater Than a Tourist – Monterey California United States:
50 Travel Tips from a Local by Katie Begley

Greater Than a Tourist – Chanai Crete Greece:
50 Travel Tips from a Local by Dimitra Papagrigoraki

Greater Than a Tourist – The Garden Route Western Cape Province
South Africa:
50 Travel Tips from a Local by Li-Anne McGregor van Aardt

Greater Than a Tourist – Sevilla Andalusia Spain:
50 Travel Tips from a Local by Gabi Gazon

Greater Than a Tourist – Kota Bharu Kelantan Malaysia:
50 Travel Tips from a Local by Aditi Shukla

Children's Book: Charlie the Cavalier Travels the World by Lisa
Rusczyk

>TOURIST

> TOURIST

Visit Greater Than a Tourist for Free Travel Tips
  http://GreaterThanATourist.com

Sign up for the Greater Than a Tourist Newsletter for
  discount days, new books, and travel information:
  http://eepurl.com/cxspyf

Follow us on Facebook for tips, images, and ideas:
  https://www.facebook.com/GreaterThanATourist

Follow us on Pinterest for travel tips and ideas:
  http://pinterest.com/GreaterThanATourist

Follow us on Instagram for beautiful travel images:
  http://Instagram.com/GreaterThanATourist

>TOURIST

> TOURIST

Please leave your honest review of this book on Amazon and Goodreads. Please send your feedback to GreaterThanaTourist@gmail.com as we continue to improve the series. Thank you. We appreciate your positive and constructive feedback. Thank you.

METRIC CONVERSIONS

TEMPERATURE

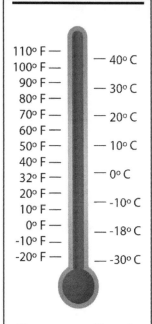

110° F —
100° F —   — 40° C
90° F —
80° F —   — 30° C
70° F —   — 20° C
60° F —
50° F —   — 10° C
40° F —
32° F —   — 0° C
20° F —
10° F —   — -10° C
0° F —
-10° F —   — -18° C
-20° F —   — -30° C

To convert F to C:

Subtract 32, and then multiply by 5/9 or .5555.

To Convert C to F:

Multiply by 1.8 and then add 32.

32F = 0C

LIQUID VOLUME

To Convert:................Multiply by
U.S. Gallons to Liters................ 3.8
U.S. Liters to Gallons 26
Imperial Gallons to U.S. Gallons 1.2
Imperial Gallons to Liters....... 4.55
Liters to Imperial Gallons 22
1 Liter = .26 U.S. Gallon
1 U.S. Gallon = 3.8 Liters

DISTANCE

To convert ....Multiply by
Inches to Centimeters 2.54
Centimeters to Inches 39
Feet to Meters...................... .3
Meters to Feet 3.28
Yards to Meters 91
Meters to Yards 1.09
Miles to Kilometers 1.61
Kilometers to Miles............ .62
1 Mile = 1.6 km
1 km = .62 Miles

WEIGHT

1 Ounce = .28 Grams
1 Pound = .4555 Kilograms
1 Gram = .04 Ounce
1 Kilogram = 2.2 Pounds

TRAVEL QUESTIONS

- Do you bring presents home to family or friends after a vacation?

- Do you get motion sick?

- Do you have a favorite billboard?

- Do you know what to do if there is a flat tire?

- Do you like a sun roof open?

- Do you like to eat in the car?

- Do you like to wear sun glasses in the car?

- Do you like toppings on your ice cream?

- Do you use public bathrooms?

- Did you bring your cell phone and does it have power?

- Do you have a form of identification with you?

- Have you ever been pulled over by a cop?

- Have you ever given money to a stranger on a road trip?

- Have you ever taken a road trip with animals?

- Have you ever went on a vacation alone?

- Have you ever run out of gas?

- If you could move to any place in the world, where would it be?

- If you could travel anywhere in the world, where would you travel?

- If you could travel in any vehicle, which one would it be?

- If you had three things to wish for from a magic genie, what would they be?

- If you have a driver's license, how many times did it take you to pass the test?

- What are you the most afraid of on vacation?

- What do you want to get away from the most when you are on vacation?

- What foods smells bad to you?

- What item to you bring on ever trip with you away from home?

- What makes you sleepy?

- What song would you love to hear on the radio when you're cruising on the highway?

- What travel job would you want the least?

- What will you miss most while you are away from home?

- What is something you always wanted to try?

- What is the best road side attraction that you ever saw?

- What is the farthest distance you ever biked?

- What is the farthest distance you ever walked?

- What is the weirdest thing you needed to buy while on vacation?

- What is your favorite candy?

- What is your favorite color car?

- What is your favorite family vacation?

- What is your favorite food in the world?

- What is your favorite gas station drink or food?

- What is your favorite license plate design?

- What is your favorite restaurant in the world?

- What is your favorite smell?

- What is your favorite song?

- What is your favorite sound that nature makes?

- What is your favorite thing to bring home from a vacation?

- What is your favorite vacation with friends?

- What is your favorite way to relax?

- What is your favorite weather conditions while driving?

- Where in the world would you rather never get to travel?

- Where is the farthest place you ever traveled in a car?

- Where is the farthest place you ever went North, South, East and West?

- Where is your favorite place in the world?

- Who is your favorite singer?

- Who taught you how to drive?

- Who will you miss the most while you are away?

- Who if the first person you will call when you get to your destination?

- Who brought you on your first vacation?

- Who likes to travel the most in your life?

- Would you rather be hot or cold?

- Would you rather drive above, below, or at the speed limited?

- Would you rather drive on a highway or a back road?

- Would you rather go on a train or a boat?

- Would you rather go to the beach or the woods?

TRAVEL BUCKET LIST

NOTES

Made in the USA
Middletown, DE
28 August 2023